GRACIE FIELDS
Her Life in Pictures

GRACIE FIELDS

Her Life in Pictures

Peter Hudson

 Robson Books

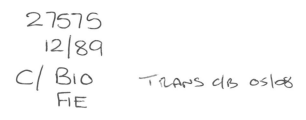
First published in Great Britain in 1989 by Robson Books Ltd,
Bolsover House, 5–6 Clipstone Street, London W1P 7EB

British Library Cataloguing in Publication Data
Gracie Fields : her life in pictures.
1. Popular music. Singing. Fields, Gracie – Biographies
I. Hudson, Peter
784.5′0092′4

ISBN 0 86051 603 2

Typeset and printed by BAS Printers Ltd, Over Wallop, Hants

Contents

Acknowledgements

I would like to thank the following people for their help on this book:

Betty Aked
Ken Appleby
Aldo Aprea
The late Lillian Aza
Morris Aza
Doreen Berrill
Irena Bounous
John Cole
The late Mary Davey
Candy D'Esposito
Brian Duff (*Daily Express*)
Elio and Gastoni Grandi
The late Neva Hecker

The late Teddy Holmes
Joan Kitchen
Margaret Legg
Eileen and Leslie McGibbon
John Offord
Grace Orbell
Patricia and Nino Pollio
S Richardson
Eddie Saunders
Mel Smith
Annette Stansfield and the late
  Tom Stansfield
Derek Warman

Introduction

The story and rise to fame of the amazing 'Gracie Fields' began in Rochdale, a small cotton town in Lancashire, on 9 January 1898, where she was born to Fred Stansfield and his wife, Jenny, above her grandmother's fish and chip shop in Molesworth Street. She was to be the eldest of four children, Edith, Betty and Tommy.

From these unlikely circumstances she reached dizzy heights, conquered every medium of entertainment, was adored and worshipped by the British people and acclaimed wherever she went, becoming one of Britain's most popular entertainers, enrapturing her audiences until her untimely death at Capri in 1979. What really made her such a popular success was the fact that, besides her talent, she never ever lost her humility and was just as natural with aristocracy as with roadsweepers. For Gracie always treated people as equals. She never ever really thought of herself as the big star that she was.

EARLY YEARS

me at the age of 1

Gracie Fields

From a very early age Grace Stansfield knew what poverty was all about. Few people in a smoky Lancashire cotton town had the means to get away from either working in the factory or other menial jobs. Grace's mother, Jenny, was stage struck and from an early age had dreamed of going on the stage but when she saw this was not possible, she pushed her talented daughter, Grace, there instead.

Almost from infancy young Grace had it instilled into her by her mother that the theatre was of paramount importance and that it was the only career for her. She was sent whenever possible to the gallery at the Rochdale Hippodrome to watch the show and learn from the performers. This was to be about the only thing she got in the way of formal training, because the Stansfield family most certainly did not have the money to pay for stage or drama classes nor did Grace's father consider it was important then. Her career really started at the age of seven when she won an amateur talent contest at the Rochdale Hippodrome.

She left Broadfield School in Rochdale, near her birthplace, after a short formal education. Her school report showed that she was at home more than at school and she said later in life, 'I often wished I'd had a better education but at the time I really wasn't interested.'

There were very few photographs taken of the Stansfield family because a visit to a photographer's studio was expensive.
Here, Jenny, a firm but protective mother, poses with Grace's sisters, Edith and Betty.

Grace, age 12, in an early juvenile troupe.
By the time she was 17, the posters
declared her to be 'Young Grace
Stansfield, Rochdale's Own Girl Vocalist'.

The facing page shows Grace (*left*) with a school friend.

Grace at 15 with her
younger brother, Tommy,
for whom she and her sisters
had a strong affection
throughout their lives.

STARTING OUT

Gracie, as she was now known, in an early
revue. In 1914 when she appeared in her first
revue, a theatre manager told her mother that
'Grace Stansfield' was too long to go in lights
over a theatre. So, 'Gracie Fields' was born.

An early publicity photograph of the kind handed round to audiences during Gracie's shows.

MISS GRACIE and her Father

Gracie with her father, Fred Stansfield, who always said that his daughter should have a nice steady job in the factory.

In 1912, age fourteen, Grace appeared in her third juvenile troupe called 'Charburn's Young Stars'. This was to be the start of her long career when she began to introduce comedy into her act, in the form of comic songs and comic monologues, such as 'The Biggest Aspidistra in the World', 'I Took My Harp to a Party' and 'The Little Pudding Basin'.

It was at this time that Gracie met up with Archie Pitt, a Cockney comedian, who invited her to join him in a revue he had compiled called *It's a Bargain* which, although not greatly successful, drew the crowds with their combined talents. Gracie never really liked Archie even though he later became her husband. Her mother, however, realized that Archie was a good showman who could enhance Gracie's career, particularly when he would cut the better songs from other members of the company to give them to her daughter.

The revue that was to change her life began in 1918. It began modestly but was to prove to be one of the most popular revues to tour the provincial theatres. During its run, in 1923, Archie Pitt and Gracie were married. Archie realized that Gracie had real star quality and was the person that audiences flocked to see and so brought in the money. He wanted to hold on to her, so marriage, if more for convenience than love, was the solution. Gracie was to say, many years later, that 'they were all black years', and she had allowed it to happen because she had only been interested in her work and future success.

In spite of her personal unhappiness, her great provincial success had given her confidence and a stage presence quite unique, as well as making both Archie and her rich. At Archie's behest, four separate companies of the revue were dispatched to the provinces, headed by Edith, Betty and Tommy, who all performed the principal roles. Most of the family joined in as managers, scenic designers and prompters.

What Gracie most needed now was a metropolitan success and when the revue, which had been touring since 1918, was booked in to London's Alhambra Theatre in 1925, it was a triumph and Gracie was proclaimed a star by the London critics. The revue — *Mr Tower of London* — had taken many years to reach London but Gracie had now arrived.

Gracie Fields

Gracie with her sisters, Edith (*left*) and Betty
(*right*). Both went on to the stage and appeared
in all Gracie's early revues.

Mr Tower of London troupe on tour in the
provinces in the mid 1920s. From left to right
are: Gracie, Archie holding the reins, Betty
wearing a white hat, and Edith.

MR. TOWER OF LONDON COMPANY.

Mr Tower of London company outside
The Palace Theatre, Halifax, Yorkshire.

A publicity photograph for *Mr Tower of London*.

After Gracie's marriage in 1923 to Archie Pitt (*left*), the man who helped to make her a star, her new husband built a vast house called The Towers in Bishops Avenue, Hampstead, London. These two photographs show the entrance sitting room and the ballroom.

Gracie in her favourite comedy part in *Mr Tower of London*. She saw herself as an entertainer, rather than just a singer, interspersing straight ballads with comedy songs in all her shows.

A STAR
SHINES BRIGHTLY

MISS GRACIE FIELDS

The four publicity photographs (*on this page and on the facing page*) were taken between 1927 and 1930, when Gracie began recording and continued to perform in revues.

Gracie Fields

For her first straight play, *SOS*, at the St James Theatre, Gracie did the rounds of London society with Sir Gerald du Maurier in an attempt to temporarily remove her Lancashire accent.

By 1926, Gracie had become a national figure, much in demand in all channels of showbusiness. It had been a struggle to get there. While acting in the early revues, she had also worked on the costumes, on drilling the dancing girls and on making up the actors. And at home, as the eldest child, she was expected to help look after her brother, sisters and ageing uncle.

Gracie's marriage to Archie Pitt had been making her unhappy for some years and they agreed to divorce in 1939. She had also not been well and, when a friend suggested she saw a doctor, she was diagnosed as having cancer. The newspapers and radio soon made her public aware of the situation and, after a long delicate operation, when it was not known whether she would live or die, she received over 250,000 letters and telegrams from her admirers all over the world.

In the revue, *Walk This Way* (*facing*) in 1931, Gracie performed to full houses every night. The programme left shows Gracie in a Manchester variety show in 1934.

Winter Garden Theatre
DRURY LANE, W.C.2
Licensed by the Lord Chamberlain to - - - WILLIAM COOPER

"WALK THIS WAY!"
A REVUE
By ARCHIE PITT

The red carpets were out for Gracie's return to Rochdale to visit an infirmary in 1934.

Later that year, Gracie went to Blackpool to film *Sing As We Go* with Lawrence Grossmith.

Arrival Home from S.A.
1934

Gracie with her mother
and father (*above*) and her
nephew, Tony Parry
(*left*), on arrival home
from her first variety tour
of South Africa.

Filming in 1935 was a family affair. Gracie's sister, Edith, (*right*) appeared with her in the film, *Queen of Hearts*. Here they shared a packet of crisps with Betty (*left*). Brother Tommy (*below, right*) joined up with Gracie in *Look Up and Laugh*.

Photographers tracked Gracie down on a visit to a hairdresser on her second tour of South Africa in 1936 (*facing*).

In 1927, Gracie paid her first visit to Capri and fell in love with it — a love that was to last all her life. This photograph shows the villa, Il Fortino, which she bought in 1933 and was later to become the famous Canzone del Mare.

Gracie was again top of the bill at the Palladium on her third visit there in 1935.

All Gracie's early films featured songs that became hits. Her first film, *Sally in Our Alley*, 1931, produced her signature tune 'Sally' and the following year saw 'Looking on the Bright Side', from the film of the same name — and a popular theme in the Depression. At the end of *The Show Goes On* in 1937 (*above*), the song, 'Smile When You Say Goodbye' always reduced the audience to tears.

At her home in Greentrees in Finchley, London, in 1937 with her parents (*above*) and with her brother-in-law, Douglas Wakefield (*right*).

Gracie began her radio career in the 1930s, her broadcasts playing a significant part in family life in the 40s and 50s. When Gracie Fields was on the air in the 1930s, Parliament was likely to be adjourned! In the photograph, she broadcasts to Australia in 1936 with Harry Parr–Davies (piano) and Basil Dean.

Although Greentrees was a favourite for family gatherings, Gracie liked The Haven at Telscombe Cliffs, near Brighton, where she eventually built bungalows for her family.

Gracie's home town, Rochdale, gave her the Freedom of the borough in May 1937. Left, she laughs with the mayor and the journalist, Hannen Swaffer.

From 1937 to 1938, Gracie was in Hollywood to publicize her forthcoming Twentieth Century-Fox contract to make the films, *We're Going to Be Rich*, *Keep Smiling* and *Shipyard Sally*. This photograph shows Gracie with Tyrone Power and the ice skater, Sonja Henie. The one below captures Shirley Temple's birthday party in Santa Monica.

Party time in Hollywood — Gracie with Harry Parr-Davies, Paulette Goddard and Monty Banks, whom she met in 1936, at a dinner party and (*left*), cutting the cake with (*left to right*) Joan Blondell, Carmen Miranda and William Bendix.

A still from the film, *We're Going to Be Rich*, made in 1937.

In 1938, Gracie was made a CBE for her contribution to British arts and showbusiness. Here she is pictured outside Buckingham Palace after the investiture by George VI.

Gracie launched the paddle steamer *SS Gracie Fields* in April 1936 — a boat she used for the children from the orphanage she founded at Peacehaven, Sussex, in 1933.

GRACIE'S
WAR YEARS

This family group shows Gracie, with young Grace, her niece, in the centre. From left to right are: Aunt Margaret, Douglas and Edith Wakefield with Douglas Junior, Dorothy and Tommy Stansfield, her parents, Betty and Roy Parry with son Tony. In the group below, Gracie cuts the cake for her nephew at his birthday party in 1941.

Gracie enjoyed everyday life in California, including shopping in Santa Monica.

On 19 March 1940, she married Monty Banks (*left*) in Santa Monica. Alfred Hitchcock (*right*) was among the special guests.

Another wedding photograph of Gracie and Monty Banks (*right*). Gracie had met Monty, an Italian farmer turned film director when she heard from a fellow actor four years earlier that he worked for a director who had 'everybody in stitches'. Gracie responded by saying, 'Bring him down to lunch at Peacehaven on Sunday'. Monty accepted, subsequently bringing laughter both to her films and to her life.

Her operation for cancer of the cervix in 1939 had been a success but had left her weak and in need of recuperation. She went with Mary Davey, her companion, and Monty, to her villa at Capri in July 1939. However, as the threat of war grew, she decided to return to England, arriving home on 1 September, just two days before war was declared. Although still supposed to be convalescing, she then went to France to entertain the BEF troops, wanting to 'do her bit', along with the comedian, Arthur Askey. In 1940, when her divorce from Archie was made absolute, she left for California to marry Monty.

In June 1940, Italy entered the war on the side of Germany, creating a huge dilemma for Gracie and her new husband. Monty, an Italian subject, was threatened with internment as an enemy alien. To avoid this and to protect her marriage, Gracie took up the offer of a series of concerts in Canada.

The British Press then began a vilification campaign against Gracie, accusing her of being a traitor and of running away in time of war. This was to leave a lasting and hurtful impression on her and her reputation. Gracie herself believed that she was helping the war effort as much as she could by earning over £500,000 in North America.

In December 1941, Japan attacked the US fleet at Pearl Harbor and the US then declared war on Japan and Germany. Gracie continued to entertain the American and Allied servicemen in the US and in the Pacific.

As the war ended, her own future looked uncertain. Her family and her marriage were safe but this could not be said of her reputation in Great Britain, although two brief war-years visits home had shown her that her public still admired her.

A dinner party in
Santa Monica with
Charlie Chaplin and
Constance Collier.

In 1941, Gracie paid a
flying visit home from
America, visiting her
friend Deenie
O'Hanlon's farm in
Prestbury, with Mary
Davey (*right*).

In 1941, Gracie bought a house, La Escondita, in Santa Monica, for her mother, whose health required a warm climate. Here they both drink tea (*centre*) with her secretary, Neva Hecker (*right*) and Monty. To the left, Gracie entertains for ENSA, with pianist and friend, Teddy Holmes.

Cleaning the windows of
La Escondita in 1941.

With her family at La Escondita in 1941. Left to right are: Sister-in-law Dorothy, Gracie and Betty. Below, a group by the swimming pool.

Although her family came to visit her in California, Gracie's sisters actually lived in England. Here Edith poses with her son, Douglas Junior, Gracie's namesake, Grace, and her husband.

'For years we had an
   Aspidistra in a flower pot,
On the What-not, near the
   hat-stand in the hall.
It didn't seem to grow, till
   one day our Brother Joe
Had a notion that he'd make
   it strong and tall . . . .'

At home in La Escondita with Monty.

The Bundles for Britain Campaign was one of Gracie's favourite charities. In this concert to raise money for sending parcels to Britain, she appeared (*left to right*) with Eleanor Roosevelt and Gertrude Lawrence.

Above, Gracie's first straight film part in 1943 involved her looking after Monty Woolley in *Holy Matrimony*.

Gracie sings the popular comedy song 'I Took My Harp to a Party and Nobody Asked Me to Play' (*left*).

My Best Wishes
Gracie
1944

Another concert tour in 1945 took Gracie to the Cocos Islands, adding yet another regimental badge to her bush hat.

Overleaf, she appeared with Basil Dean (*left*) in a wartime concert tour of Ceylon.

Gracie entertained the
officers and men in the
Pacific, gaining followers
wherever she went.

On their way home to Capri — Gracie and Monty in Naples in 1945.

What a wonderful day The Wars Over just as we near Bougainville. May be will get home a bit quicker Bestest love to you from Uncle Mario & yes Aunty Grace

The war was over but Gracie visited the wounded in hospitals throughout the United States. On the facing page Gracie talks to a young soldier in Chicago.

STILL THE
GREATEST STAR

In 1945, Gracie returned to her favourite home at Capri, which had been occupied by American troops during the war, with Monty. She began to rebuild the house and the estate, adding terraces and about 50 bungalows for her visitors and family.

Until 1950, when Monty died suddenly on the Orient Express after a Christmas visit to Gracie's family in England, Gracie's time was occupied by tours of Australia and New Zealand in 1945, return visits to England for a radio series *Gracie's Working Parties* and, in 1948, for a variety show at the Palladium. Knowing this appearance would test her postwar popularity in Britain, Gracie was understandably nervous. She opened with 'Take Me to Your Heart Again' and by the end of the evening, there was not a dry eye in the house. Gracie had made a triumphant return. 1951 saw her as the star of the Festival of Variety at the Royal Albert Hall, which was part of the Festival of Britain celebrations, before she returned to Capri, bereft by Monty's death.

These two photographs show Gracie with her American secretary, Neva Hecker, on holiday in Canada (*above*) and with her manager, brother-in-law and friend, Bert Aza (*facing*) in 1945.

Gracie's favourite nephew, Michael Stansfield, with brother Tommy.

Monty stands on the terrace of Il Fortino in 1947, with the Faraglioni Rocks in the background.

Gracie sings in the
chairlift to Monte Solario
on Capri in 1948.

A gradual transformation
was taking place at Il
Fortino as Gracie created
a luxury bathing complex
and restaurant. It was to
be renamed La Canzone
del Mare (The Song of
the Sea) and to become a
popular rendezvous for
the rich smart set
of Europe.

Facing, a publicity still taken in 1947.

A portrait taken by Dorothy Wilding in 1949.

Gracie returned to Rochdale again to give a concert in 1949 (*top, facing left*). A night out with the family (*below left*) captures (*front, left to right*): Cynthia (Tommy's wife), Mrs Stansfield, Gracie, Douglas and Edith Wakefield, Edward Saunders. *Back*, Tommy, Monty and Betty Saunders.

The photograph above with Monty was taken for publicity purposes by Dorothy Wilding in 1949.

Gracie maintained The Haven at Telscombe Cliffs, near Brighton, as her main family home in England. It was here that the family gathered at weekends, with Gracie, whenever possible.

THE
LATE YEARS

One day Gracie's record player broke down. Her nephew, Tony Parry, knew a fellow islander, Boris Alperovici, who was good with electrical equipment, and invited him to the villa to see what he could do. At first, Gracie did not take too much notice of him as he did not appear to speak any English. When she discovered that he did, she invited him to lunch. He became a frequent visitor over the next few months and she grew quite fond of this shy man. On 18 February 1952, they were married in the Catholic Church at Capri (*bottom, facing left*). The photograph above (*facing left*) shows Boris and Gracie in 1954 with the family on the terrace of Canzone del Mare and, in the one above, sister Edith joins Gracie and Boris in Brighton.

Gracie's sister Betty was a painter and sculptor. Here she works on a model of Gracie's head.

Gracie and her father in the piazza at Capri in 1951.

Gracie made her first TV play with *The Old Lady Shows Her Medals* in the United States. This was followed by *Mrs Harris Goes to Paris* and *A Tale of Two Cities* (*above*) with Michael Gough and Denholm Elliott. Right, with a good book at her agent's house in Maida Vale, London, in 1953.

The Canzone del Mare was now complete, Boris having
helped her with the last stages. The lavish setting drew
Gracie's admirers from all over the world. Here she is
pictured with English visitors (*above*). Others included
Maria Callas, the Kennedys, Aristotle Onassis, Greta Garbo,
Noël Coward, King Farouk, Sarah Churchill and Christiaan
Barnard — all of whom spent their leisure time in the
Canzone. To the left, Gracie poses near the restaurant.

Mario Pollio (*left*) was Gracie's caretaker at the Canzone and Lord and Lady Kitchen (*centre, below*) were island neighbours.

Gracie was invited to no less than ten Royal Variety Command Performances between 1928 and 1978. In 1964 (*above*), she chats to the Queen and Lord Delfont.

A party in Capri in 1964
with David Rawnsley, the
potter (*right*).

Gracie's tour to Australia
in 1965 (*left*) gave her an
opportunity to meet up
with her sister, Betty,
who then lived in
Melbourne.

Singing 'If I Had a Hammer' as she opens the Vitool Factory in 1970 on the site of her birthplace in Rochdale. *Below*, at the Canzone del Mare.

At Capri, Gracie sings at
a party in 1973, poses
with the ballet dancer,
John Gilpin, and is a
special guest at the
wedding of one of her
carpenters in 1974.

CAPRI - 1974.

OUR LOVE & GoodWishes
FOR A HAPPY CHRISTMAS
AND NEW YEAR

Gracie

A Christmas card to the
author in 1974.

Gracie's sister, Betty, and
her husband visit Gracie
and Boris in 1974.

By 1975, Gracie's visits to The Haven became less frequent. Mary Davey (*left*), previously her companion, had become caretaker of The Haven in the 50s and Tommy, her brother, had retired near by. Below, she and Boris pose with Tommy's wife and children.

The estate of Canzone del Mare in the 70s: the south front of the main villa (*above*); Gracie on the south front terrace (*right*); the sign at the entrance of the estate (*facing*) and the swimming pool and restaurant (*below right*).

'Best love to young Grace
from old Grace 1977'.

Gracie visited Bing Crosby in nearby Brighton in October 1977, just after his last concert.

Two photographs taken of Gracie in December 1977 — with children on the island (*above*)
and with husband Boris (*facing*).

Singing 'Sally' in Rochdale in September 1978 when she opened the Gracie Fields Theatre for her 80th birthday (*facing left*). Above, she talks to Sandy Powell just before her final concert in Rochdale.

Gracie unveils the plaque
(*right*) inside the Gracie
Fields Theatre (*above*).

THIS PLAQUE COMMEMORATES
THE NAMING OF THIS THEATRE AS
THE GRACIE FIELDS THEATRE,
OULDER HILL,
IN HONOUR OF ROCHDALE'S MOST
FAMOUS DAUGHTER, ON THE
OCCASION OF HER 80TH BIRTHDAY,
JANUARY 9TH 1978.

ARCHITECTS
THE GREENHALGH & WILLIAMS
PARTNERSHIP
1978

After her last concert in Rochdale, Gracie celebrates with (*left to right*) Ben Warris, Larry Grayson and Sandy Powell.

Before she left the North, she was invited to be guest of honour of the Variety Club of Great Britain, at a special luncheon in Manchester, where she was given a Silver Heart for her contribution to helping handicapped children, and a Golden Disc, by Warwick Records, for her contribution to the record industry. In November, she was the 'surprise item' at the end of the Royal Variety Show, where she received a standing ovation and reduced many of the audience to tears. She was 80 years old and a British Institution.

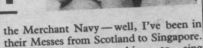

TOP OF
WARRIOR SQ.

ELITE

ST. LEONARDS

TALKIE THEATRE

MANAGER; L; LOVELL;

'PHONE 282

MONDAY, NOVEMBER 14TH; AND DURING WEEK

ENGLAND'S GREATEST ENTERTAINER

Gracie FIELDS in
LOOKING on the BRIGHT SIDE

MIRTH AND MELODY!

Another gloriously British Film that definitely cheers one up.

Hear Gracie in her best form sing

"AFTER TONIGHT WE SAY GOODBYE"
"YOU'RE MORE THAN ALL THE WORLD TO ME"
"HE'S DEAD BUT HE WON'T LIE DOWN"

ALSO

FORGOTTEN WOMAN

FEATURING

MARION SHILLING and REX BELL

JUST AN INTERESTING HUMAN STORY

WE'RE GOING TO BE RICH

GRACIE FIELDS

VICTOR McLAGLEN

Gracie was a great dog lover.
Sandy, with Gracie's housekeeper,
Irena (*above*), disliked Italian men
and therefore proved to be an
excellent guard dog. To the right,
Gracie, aged 81 and now a Dame,
sits outside her house in Anacapri,
built in the 60s as an escape from
the Canzone del Mare, which was
crowded with visitors in the
summer and very cold in winter.

In July 1979, Gracie developed pneumonia and was taken to hospital in Naples, coming home to Capri in August. She died on 27 September at the Canzone del Mare and was buried in the Non-Catholic Cemetery, just a short journey from her home. All the people of Capri came to their gates to pay tribute to a great lady and friend, the pallbearers being waiters who worked in her restaurant.

Best Wishes
Gracie Fields

The world mourned the loss of a truly great entertainer. Gracie Fields was someone special —
unique, and now a legend of British showbusiness.

A Brief Biography

9 January 1898   Gracie Fields, born Rochdale, Lancashire, as Grace Stansfield

1912   Appeared in first juvenile troupe, Charburn's Young Stars

1914   Met Archie Pitt

1914   Appeared in her first revue, *Yes I Think So*

1916   Revue, *It's a Bargain*

1918   Start of the revue, *Mr Tower of London*

1923   Married Archie Pitt, who helped make her a star

1925   Revue, *By Request*

1925   *Mr Tower of London* opened at the Alhambra Theatre, Leicester Square — Gracie was then proclaimed a star

1927   Paid her first visit to Capri

1928   Started her recording career

1 March 1928   Appeared in her first Royal Command Performance

1928   Appeared with Sir Gerald du Maurier in the play, *SOS* at St James Theatre

1929   Revue, *The Show's the Thing*

1930   Paid her first visit to the USA

1931   Revue, *Walk This Way*

11 May 1931   Royal Variety Performance

1931   Made her first film, *Sally in Our Alley*

1932   Made film, *Looking on the Bright Side*

1933   Bought villa at Capri, Il Fortino, at Marina Piccola — later to become the Canzone del Mare

1933   Opened and founded the Gracie Fields Orphanage at Peacehaven, Sussex

1933   Made film, *This Week of Grace*

February 1933   Made her Four Millionth Record for the HMV company

1934   Made one of her most popular films, *Sing As We Go*

1934   Toured South Africa

1934   Made film, *Love, Life and Laughter*

1935   Made film, *Look Up and Laugh*

1935   Met Monty Banks

1936   Made popular film, *Queen of Hearts*

1936   Toured South Africa

8 April 1936   Launched the paddle steamer, *SS Gracie Fields*

May 1937   Was given the Freedom of her home town, Rochdale

1937   Went to Hollywood to publicize a contract with Twentieth Century-Fox films

1937   Made the popular film, *We're Going to Be Rich* with Victor McLaglen

1937   Made film, *The Show Goes On*

15 November 1937   Royal Variety Performance

1938   Received the CBE from King George VI

1938   Made film, *Keep Smiling*

28 October 1938   Appeared in all British tribute night, in aid of the London Hospital, at the Royal Albert Hall

1938   Was given the Order of Officer Sister of St John of Jerusalem

21 July 1939   Divorce from Archie Pitt

1939   Made the popular film, *Shipyard Sally* with Sydney Howard

1939   Had operation for cancer of the cervix, at the Chelsea Women's Hospital

1939   After operation went to Capri with Monty Banks and companion, Mary Davey, to convalesce

3 September 1939   War was declared

1940   Divorce from Archie Pitt became absolute

19 March 1940   Married Monty Banks

1941   Concerts in USA and Canada in aid of Britain's war effort

1942   Starred in the Broadway Vaudeville Show, *Top Notchers*

1943   Made film, *Holy Matrimony*, with Monty Woolley

1943   Appeared in film *Stage Door Canteen*, with a host of other stars

1945   Toured Australia and New Zealand

1945   Made film, *Mollie and Me*, with Monty Woolley and Roddy McDowall

1946   Made film, *Paris Underground*, with Constance Bennett

1947   Made series of radio programmes for the BBC, *Gracie's Working Parties*

3 November 1947   Royal Variety Performance

1948   Made a triumphant return to the London Palladium

September 1949   Appeared in Midnight Matinée Charity Show at London Coliseum

1950   On return to Italy from England, Monty Banks had heart attack and died

13 November 1950   Royal Variety Performance

1951   Gracie was star of Festival of Variety at the Royal Albert Hall to celebrate the Festival of Britain

29 October 1951   Royal Variety Performance

18 February 1952   Married Boris Alperovici, at Capri

3 November 1952   Royal Variety Performance

1953   Successful variety season at London Palladium

1955   Appeared in J M Barrie's play, *The Old Lady Shows Her Medals*, on American TV

1955   Was given the Silvana Award for her performance in *The Old Lady Shows Her Medals*

18 November 1957   Royal Variety Performance

1958   Had huge success with recording of Victor Young's 'Around the World'

1959   Recorded 'Little Donkey'

1964   Had successful English tour

2 November 1964   Royal Variety Performance

January 1965   Appeared on the Jack Parr show in USA

1965   Toured Australia and New Zealand

1965   Had 'sell-out' concert at the Lewisohn Stadium, New York

November 1968   Appeared at the Batley Variety Club in Yorkshire

1970   Opened new factory at Rochdale on site of her birthplace

November 1970   First appearance on the TV programme, *Stars on Sunday*

1975   Came to England to make what was to be her last LP — *The Golden Years of Gracie Fields*

1977   Special guest on Michael Parkinson show
16 September 1978   Was invited to open the Gracie Fields Theatre at Rochdale
1978   Was guest of honour at the Variety Club of Great Britain, special 80th birthday luncheon at the Midland Hotel, Manchester
13 November 1978   Royal Variety Performance as special surprise guest at the end of the show
20 February 1979   Gracie Fields became Dame Commander of the British Empire
July 1979   Was taken to the International Hospital at Naples with pneumonia
27 September 1979   Died at her home La Canzone del Mare at Capri, age 81 years
29 September 1979   Buried in the Non-Catholic cemetery at Capri

List of Personalities and Friends

Boris Alperovici
Arthur Askey
Bert Aza
Lillian Aza
Monty Banks (Bianchi)
William Bendix
Constance Bennett
Joan Blondell
Irena Bounous
Coral Browne
Maria Callas
Charlie Chaplin
Sarah Churchill
Constance Collier
Noël Coward
Bing Crosby
(Ding) Leon Davey
Mary Davey
Basil Dean
Bernard Delfont
Richard Dolman
Brian Donleavy
Sir Gerald du Maurier
HM Queen Elizabeth II
Denholm Elliott
King Farouk (of Egypt)

Greta Garbo
HM King George VI
John Gilpin
Michael Gough
Larry Grayson
George Grossmith
Neva Hecker
Sonja Henie
Alfred Hitchcock
Teddy Holmes
Lena Horne
the Kennedys
Sir Geoffrey Kitchen
Lady Joan Kitchen
Gertrude Lawrence
Margaret Livesey (Aunt)
Victor McLaglen
Carmen Miranda
Billy Nelson
Bob Newhart
Deenie O'Hanlon
Aristotle Onassis
Harry Parr-Davies
Roy Parry
Tony Parry
Archie Pitt (Sellinger)

Margarita Pollio
Mario Pollio
Sandy Powell
Tyrone Power
David Rawnsley
Cynthia Rawson
Eleanor Roosevelt
Betty Saunders
Edward Saunders
Giuseppe Savarese ('Scarola')
Annette Stansfield
Fred Stansfield
Michael Stansfield
Sarah Stansfield
Tommy Stansfield
Hannen Swaffer
Shirley Temple
Dougie Wakefield
Douglas Wakefield (Junior)
Edith Wakefield
Grace Wakefield (now Orbell)
Ben Warris
Dorothy Whiteside
Dorothy Wilding
Monty Woolley